The Story of JACOB, RACHEL, & LEAH

Genesis 27:46—29:28 for children

Written by Yvonne Halloway McCall
Illustrated by Obata Designs, Inc., by Alice Hausner

Former title: The Farmer Takes a Wife

ARCH BOOKS

Copyright © 1975, 1986 CONCORDIA PUBLISHING HOUSE
3558 S. JEFFERSON AVENUE, ST. LOUIS, MO 63118-3968
MANUFACTURED IN THE UNITED STATES OF AMERICA

ISBN 0-570-06205-5

Jacob peeked through the goatskin door,
For his parents were having
A council of war.
The problem in question
They had to decide
Was where to find Jacob a suitable bride.

"There isn't *one* in all of the land,"
His mother said, with a wave of her hand.
"There are plenty of girls
Like the one next door,
But Canaanite women are really a bore."

So they called him in,
And his father said,
"Jacob, we think it's time you were wed.
In a distant land, your mother's brother
Has a couple of daughters.
Take one or the other."

It was a long, long way
For a bridal hunt,
And he wondered just which
Of the two he would want.

He eagerly packed and went on his way
And slept in a field
At the end of the day.

He dreamed of a ladder
That rose to the sky,
Reaching from earth
to heaven on high.

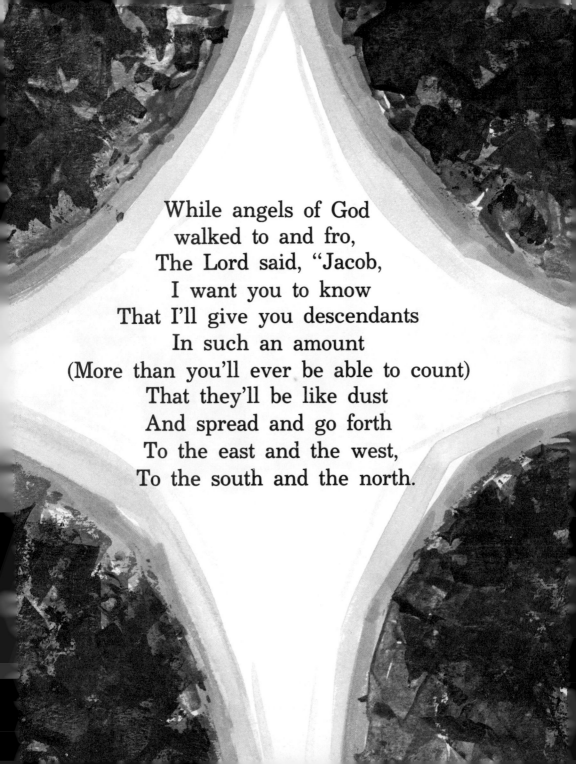

While angels of God
walked to and fro,
The Lord said, "Jacob,
I want you to know
That I'll give you descendants
In such an amount
(More than you'll ever be able to count)
That they'll be like dust
And spread and go forth
To the east and the west,
To the south and the north.

And I'll take you safely upon your way."
So Jacob continued early next day,
Over the rocky hills and the sand,
Till he came to a faraway eastern land.

He stopped by some shepherds
And smiled as he did,
For he spotted their well
With a stone for a lid.

"Water your sheep," he advised,
"Go ahead."
"We can't. We must wait
For the others," they said.

Suddenly then they hushed their talk,
For a barefoot girl,
Who was tending a flock,
Appeared on the road as golden as sun.
"That's Laban's daughter, Rachel," said one.

Jacob rolled the stone
   from the brink
All by himself,
   so her flock could drink.

As he watched her leave,
He wistfully sighed.
How could he get her to be his bride?

He met her father and sister, Leah,
And helped on their farm
Till he got an idea.
"Seven years, I'll work for you,
Uncle," he said,
"If you'll give me your daughter
Rachel to wed."

Leah was jealous,
For she loved him too,
But only the beautiful Rachel would do.
He loved her so that the years went fast,
And he worked in the fields
Till the time had passed.

And because of Jacob, Laban knew,
The number of cattle grew and grew,
And Laban got richer than ever before,
But still he wanted more and more.

His narrowed eyes began to gleam,
And Jacob never suspected his scheme.

Laban proclaimed a wedding feast
The merriest party in all the East

Everyone smiled
As the veiled young bride
Stood in her place at Jacob's side.

Jacob was happy on his wedding night,
But he gasped as he saw
In the morning light
That the girl he had married
In the banquet hall
Was the daughter Leah,
Not Rachel at all.

He stormed to Laban.
"You cheated!" he cried,

"And gave me your older
daughter as bride!"

Laban snickered. His trick had worked.
"Oh, didn't I tell you?"
He asked as he smirked.

"A younger daughter must always wait
Till her older sister finds a mate.
So I couldn't have given
You Rachel to wed.
I *had* to switch and give Leah instead.

But don't worry, nephew,"
Said Laban, said he.
"Just work for me seven
More years for free,
And you can have Rachel to marry too."
So that was what Jacob was forced to do.

Still, Jacob remembered
That long ago night
And how God said the whole thing
Would turn out all right.

DEAR PARENTS:

Some days just nothing seems to go right. But think how Jacob must have felt when he woke up and discovered he'd married the wrong girl! All of us—children and grown-ups alike—occasionally feel that our lives are a hopeless muddle. But imagine facing fourteen years of unpaid labor just to marry the right girl!

Jacob had a rough time of it all right. But he also had a source of strength to see him through, a source we all share—God's promise that everything will turn out all right. Or, as St. Paul says, "We know that in everything God works for good with those who love Him, who are called according to His purpose." (Romans 8:28) Because of Jesus' death and resurrection, this promise is ours. We can stake our lives on it.

After the children have finished with Jacob's story, read them Romans 8:28. And when problems arise in their own lives, problems which seem insoluble at the time, remind them of that promise that is theirs, the promise that will always be kept.

THE EDITOR